Original title:
In the Land of Gingerbread

Copyright © 2024 Creative Arts Management OÜ
All rights reserved.

Author: Jaxon Kingsley
ISBN HARDBACK: 978-9916-90-854-9
ISBN PAPERBACK: 978-9916-90-855-6

Celestial Confections

In a breeze of sugar fluff,
Marshmallow clouds soar up high,
Gumdrop trees refuse to budge,
As licorice vines twist and tie.

The town square's a candy maze,
Where lollipops stand tall and proud,
But watch out for gum-chewing cars,
They honk sweet tunes to the crowd.

The frosting fountain flows with glee,
Chocolate rains drizzle and dance,
But be careful not to slip,
Or end up in a candy trance!

Gingersnap squirrels prance on roofs,
Trading secrets with frosted mice,
While jellybean birds chirp in tune,
Singing songs of candy delights.

Confectionery Echoes in Moonlight

Beneath the stars, the sweets all cheer,
A cookie band plays tunes so near.
Gumdrops dancing in sugar skies,
With icing smiles and candy eyes.

Whispers of fudge float on the breeze,
As chocolate squirrels prank the trees.
Marshmallow clouds bounce overhead,
Frosting fairies dream in bed.

Lollipops and Dreams of Youth

Lollipops spin in the twilight glow,
As gummy bears put on a show.
Bouncy jelly beans hop with flair,
Twirling ribbons of candy hair.

Sour sprays in a burst of fun,
While syrup swirls around the sun.
Dreams of candy—just take a bite,
Youthful giggles fill the night.

The Spice Merchant's Lullaby

With a sprinkle of cinnamon, close your eyes,
The licorice dreams begin to rise.
A touch of nutmeg, a dash of fun,
Sugarplum tales have just begun.

Caramel streams drape like a quilt,
In a world where sweets are built.
The spice merchant hums a tune so sweet,
As gingerbread houses tap their feet.

Heralds of the Sweet Winter

Winter whispers through candy canes,
Where peppermint laughter softly reigns.
Chilly snowflakes made of icing,
Each sprinkle seems to be enticing.

Frosty windows with chocolate seams,
Covering the land in sugary dreams.
As marshmallows glide on frosty streams,
Sweet heralds giggle, bursting at seams.

The Enchanted Baker

Once there was a baker named Jim,
Whose cakes would wobble on a whim.
He'd add some sprinkles, a dash of flair,
Then send his desserts up in the air!

Cookies would dance and dance some more,
While pies would giggle, what a score!
The doughnut holes would leap and prance,
Turning every bite into a chance!

Tales from the Spice Cottage

In a cottage filled with spices and cheer,
Ginger and nutmeg would twirl in sheer!
The cinnamon sticks would play hide and seek,
While peppercorns rolled, so sly and cheek!

A cookie jar held tales like a tome,
With stories of sugar and a dash of foam.
The brownies plotted a sprinkle attack,
While marshmallows giggled, never looking back!

Biscuit Boulevard

On Biscuit Boulevard, the fun draws near,
With cookie cars honking, full of cheer.
Tarts zoom by on frosting-filled bikes,
While chocolate bars race, oh what delight!

The jellybeans cheer from the sidewalks wide,
As lollipops dance with candy in stride.
A pie-shaped bus rolls on by with a grin,
Where every slice is guaranteed to win!

Cinnamon Skies

Under skies of cinnamon and spice,
The pastries twinkled, oh so nice!
Breadsticks twirled like ballerina dreams,
While cupcakes giggled, bursting at the seams!

The cotton candy clouds floated up high,
With marshmallow puffs drifting by.
Laughter bubbled, sweet and spry,
As cakes would sing a sugary lullaby!

Whispers of Confection

In a realm where jellybeans sing,
Candy canes dance in a sugary fling.
Chocolate rivers flow, what a sight!
Marshmallow clouds fluff up the night.

Lollipop trees sway with delight,
Bubbles of gum burst, oh what a fright!
Gingerbread men chase with a grin,
While frosting fairies twirl to begin.

Crumbs of Enchanted Echoes

The cake pops giggle, oh what a tease,
Gummy bears chuckle with savory ease.
Swirls of fondant paint the air bright,
Sugar plum dreams dangle in flight.

A pie whispered secrets, warm and sweet,
With pies in the sky, what a fun treat!
Crumbs on the carpet tell stories old,
Of sweets and laughs, all tales retold.

Frosted Wishes

A scoop of delight on a cone so high,
Sprinkles shower down, oh me, oh my!
Whipped cream swirls in a dance of fun,
As cherry toppings glow in the sun.

Cookies in pajamas, ready to bake,
Giggles erupt with each silly mistake.
Sugar dust storms float in the air,
With frosting laughter, without a care.

The Cookie Castle

A fortress of cookies, tall and round,
Where licorice knights dance on the ground.
Pretzel towers stand, quite absurd,
As candy corn flags flap without a word.

Marzipan moats brim with cheer,
While jellybean dragons swoop down near.
In cookie keep, the giggles roll,
With sugar hot springs, pure joy in the bowl.

A Journey Through Candy Trails

Candy canes bend and sway,
Lollipop trees in disarray.
Chocolate rivers flow at will,
Marshmallow hills, a sticky thrill.

Gummy bears dance in the sun,
Singing songs, just having fun.
Peppermint winds blow so sweet,
Join the parade, it can't be beat!

Licorice bridges twist and twine,
Sugar-coated paths, all divine.
Jellybean smiles adorn each face,
Let's bounce along this tasty place.

With every step, a crunch and cheer,
Cupcake clouds of frosting near.
A joyous trek through sugar dreams,
A candy world is bursting at the seams.

Melting Midwinter Magic

Winter's chill melts with a grin,
Frosting snowflakes spin and spin.
Sugarplum faeries laugh and play,
Sipping cocoa, bright as day.

Taffy pulls trees, stretching high,
Fudgey squirrels wink and fly.
Caramel suns hang in the sky,
Join the fun, just give it a try!

Giggling snowmen, sprightly jolly,
Chasing shadows, oh so folly.
Marzipan flames in cheerful flares,
Bouncing through the sweet-scented airs.

Here, each moment brings delight,
Candy stars twinkling through the night.
A whimsical world, never stark,
In this place, we leave our mark.

The Wizardry of Sweets

Wizards weave with candy charms,
Jellybean magic, oh so warm.
Chocolate spells, they're quite a sight,
Syrupy potions that bubble bright.

Lollipops twirl, casting some glee,
Gummy frogs hopping here and free.
Whirling, twirling, all in a mix,
Sugar spells, using candy tricks.

Wand made of licorice, oh so neat,
Conjuring treats with crafty feat.
Cotton candy clouds drift around,
In this magic, joy is found.

Each sprinkle of sugar, a wish for fun,
A sugary battle, just begun.
The wizard beckons, come take a bite,
In a world where all feels right.

Gingerbread Whimsy

Crispy houses, frosting bright,
Candy windows, pure delight.
Gingerbread men with giggly grins,
Racing down, let the fun begin!

Spicy aromas fill the air,
Gummy pets prance without a care.
Chocolates dance, a twirl and spin,
Who knew sweets could feel like a win?

Sugar-sprinkled dreams take flight,
Nutty nods in the starlit night.
With each bite, a laughter shared,
Magical flavors that we dared.

Fondant frolics and gummy cheer,
Join the whimsy, lose all fear.
In this land where giggles dwell,
A candy-coated, joyous spell.

Gingerbread Houses and Lost Dreams

The walls are made of candy, oh what a sight,
Each door is a cookie, oh, what delight.
But once they were built, they started to sway,
A bite from a child, almost took them away.

Now leaning and wobbling, all in a row,
The roofs dripped with icing, a sticky flow.
Once proud little homes, now puddles of glee,
The taste of sweet dreams, devoured by spree.

Frosting Rivers and Chocolate Hills

A river of frosting flows down the lane,
Chocolate hills rise, but bring on the rain.
With marshmallow boats we paddle along,
We sing with the sugar, a very sweet song.

But watch for the sprinkles, they might just attack,
They scatter like ninjas, no turning back.
With laughter and giggles, we roll down the slopes,
In a world full of sweetness, we dream all our hopes.

Sugar Fairies Dance at Dusk

Sugar fairies twirl, in the twilight glow,
Sprinkling their magic, a sugary show.
They ride on gumdrops, with giggles and cheer,
Their whimsical laughter is all that you hear.

With jellybean wands, they cast little spells,
Creating a ruckus that rings like clear bells.
As the sun sets low, they flit to and fro,
In a world made of candy, their secrets will flow.

The Nutmeg Nook of Wonder

In the nutmeg nook, where the secrets hide,
Spices and sweets meet, a joyous tide.
With cinnamon giggles and clove-scented fun,
This nook of delight makes everyone run.

Just be careful, my friend, of the gingerbread cat,
Who stalks with a smirk and a fluffy little hat.
In this magical place, adventures abound,
Where laughter and sweetness forever astound.

Sweet Dreams of Confection

Candy clouds fluff in the sky,
Where gummy bears learn to fly.
Chocolate rivers swirl and swing,
While lollipops dance and sing.

Giggles echo through the halls,
As jelly beans bounce off the walls.
Cupcake castles with frosting high,
In this kingdom where sweets never die.

Marshmallow pillows, soft and warm,
Silly squirrels always in form.
No worry here, just fun and cheer,
In a world where candy is near.

The Ginger Man's Wistful Waltz

A ginger man twirls with a grin,
Doing laps with a wink and spin.
He trips on a gumdrop, oh what a sight,
Bouncing back, still full of delight.

His frosting coat shines in the sun,
Every dance move, oh what fun!
Jelly buttons sewn with care,
He wobbles on, without a care.

Tootsie rolls join in the dance,
They swirl together in a trance.
With a lollipop for a hat,
He leads them all, imagine that!

Cinnamon Whispers on the Breeze

Cinnamon swirls, a fragrant tease,
Carried softly on the breeze.
Cookie scents weave through the air,
Making everyone stop and stare.

Bakers chuckle, flour flies high,
With silly hats and apple pie.
Their spatulas wave, they shout with glee,
As cupcakes leap, wild and free.

Sprinkles rain down like confetti bright,
Colorful chaos, a pure delight.
Whisking dreams with each sweet swirl,
In this place of joy, where giggles unfurl.

Cookie Crumbs and Sugar Trails

Tiny footprints in the flour,
Every corner, a sweetened power.
Cookie crumbs scatter with pride,
As sweet treats take a fun-filled ride.

Silly ants, they hastily march,
Building villages, great and arch.
With licorice ladders, they ascend,
On candy cane bridges, round the bend.

A jolly pie rolls down the lane,
While frosting rivers swell with gain.
Giggles bubble, laughter prevails,
In this land of cookie crumbs and trails.

You Are My Sweet Haven

In a house made of cream,
Where gumdrops shine bright,
Chocolate rivers do gleam,
And everything feels right.

The roof is a waffle,
With icing so sweet,
A marshmallow soft,
Where my dreamers retreat.

Candy lights twinkle,
Like stars in the night,
In my sweet little space,
Everything's just right.

With jellybean friends,
We giggle and play,
In this sugary land,
We'll dance all day!

The Sugar Fairy's Dance

A fairy with sprinkles,
Is ready to twirl,
With a hop and a skip,
She gives it a whirl.

Cupcakes do cheer,
As frosting takes flight,
In a flamboyant jig,
That dazzles the night.

Lollipops join in,
With a rhythm so sweet,
Footloose and fancy,
They'll dance on their feet.

With a giggle and grin,
They flutter and sway,
In a sugary world,
Where sweets laugh and play!

Delights from the Cookie Jar

In the jar on the shelf,
Lie treasures galore,
Chocolate chips stacked high,
Who could ask for more?

Oatmeal and raisins,
Each cookie a treat,
A munch or a crunch,
Makes life feel so sweet.

The giggles they share,
When a crumb hits the floor,
Even crumbs have a party,
And beg for some more!

So dip into the joy,
And nibble with glee,
For every little bite,
Is a taste of pure glee!

Whimsical Whiskers

There's a cat with a hat,
Made of spun sugar bliss,
With whiskers of candy,
You can't help but miss!

He prances and pounces,
With frosted delight,
Chasing dreams in the air,
From morning to night.

His tail is a twist,
Of licorice strong,
In this funny old world,
Is where he belongs.

With each playful leap,
He dances so sly,
In a swirl of sweet fun,
As he catches the sky!

Caramel Rivers

On a boat of chocolate fudge,
We float down sweet streams,
Gummy bears waving hello,
In our candy-coated dreams.

Riding waves of syrup flow,
Popcorn clouds fluff above,
Giggling fish will jump and play,
Socks made of marshmallow love.

Where jellybeans splash around,
Each splash is a burst of cheer,
Bubblegum fish sing in tune,
Their laughter we hold dear.

With rainbow sails we steer ahead,
Sailing strong and true,
On caramel rivers, joys ahead,
With a crew of sugar, too.

Sugar Plum Reverie

In fields of sweet sugar grass,
Bouncing with cheerful glee,
Sugar plums play hide and seek,
Underneath a candy tree.

Lollipop birds serenade,
With notes that swirl and twirl,
As chocolate raindrops tumble down,
Creating a cocoa whirl.

Dancing fairies all around,
With wings of crisp taffy,
They giggle and twirl, oh what joy,
In this sugary little happy.

Dreamers hop from cloud to cloud,
With all their sweet delight,
In a world of fun and giggles,
Under stars that shine so bright.

Dreaming of Ginger Houses

Brick by brick, we build our dreams,
With frosting on the top,
Making roofs of crispy cheers,
In this candy land, we hop.

Gingerbread men on patrol,
Guarding all our treats,
Waving cookies from the walls,
As the icing rainbows greet.

Imagining a spin and dance,
On licorice-laden floors,
Where gumdrops light up every glance,
And truffles line the doors.

Tickled by the sweet aromas,
Of minty breezes flowing,
We'll feast till laughter fills the air,
In ginger dreams, we're glowing.

Marzipan Meadows

In meadows where the nutty blooms,
Marzipan flowers sway,
Sticky fingers pluck them quick,
In the sunshine's golden ray.

Bouncing bunnies made of cake,
Chase after candy bees,
With flowers of bright jelly rolls,
That sway upon the breeze.

Rockets made of licorice full,
Launch us up to skies,
Where taffy moons and stars all shine,
As sugar-coated pie.

With creamy clouds above our heads,
And breezes sweetly blown,
In a world of marzipan cheer,
We'll never feel alone.

Whirling Fancies of Flour

A cloud of dust, oh what a sight,
The kitchen spins, in morning light.
Rolling pins dance a merry jig,
While sugar sprinkles on a big pig.

Eggs start cracking, shells take flight,
A flour tornado in sheer delight.
Sift and swirl, a frothy sea,
Baking dreams of fun for thee.

Laughter bubbles, a jovial mix,
As ginger folks strut their dancing tricks.
Whisked away on a sweetened breeze,
Creating chaos, all with ease.

Cookies wink and cupcakes tease,
Chocolate rivers trickle with ease.
In this kingdom where giggles crop,
We bake and play, we'll never stop.

Beneath the Icing Veil

A frosty crown on gingerbread heads,
With candy jewels upon their beds.
Marshmallow fluff clouds pass by,
As sprinkles tumble from the sky.

Young ones giggle, old ones grin,
At the green gumdrop wearing a fin.
The frosting flows like rivers wide,
Beneath the icing, joy can't hide.

Gumdrop castles and lollipop trees,
Each bite tickles, such joyous tease.
Chocolate rivers swirl and bend,
In dessert dreams, we never end.

With each sweet crumb, funny tales,
Of licorice highways and cookie trails.
Beneath this glaze, we play with glee,
In a world of sweets, just you and me.

The Warmth of Cinnamon

A dash of spice, a pinch of glee,
Cinnamon swirls, come dance with me.
The oven hums a merry tune,
As cookies rise beneath the moon.

The scent of joy fills up the room,
With giggles bouncing, like lilting bloom.
Sticky fingers, a floury mess,
But laughter reigns, we won't confess.

Nutmeg whispers jokes in the air,
As sugar smiles, without a care.
In every bite, a burst of cheer,
The warmth of spice brings everyone near.

Each crumb a giggle, every taste a fun,
Together we bask in the golden sun.
With every sprinkle, we take a chance,
In this funny feast, let's dance, let's dance!

Spiced Tales of Wonder

Once upon a doughy lore,
Where sugar dreams dance on the floor.
Ginger giants with icing hats,
Tell tales of cookies, and silly cats.

Caramel rivers, all sticky and sweet,
Greeted by mice on a cookie sheet.
Spiced mahogany and peppermint beams,
Frosted laughter fills our dreams.

A waltz with a peanut butter queen,
Chasing marshmallows, what a scene!
Through candy forests we twist and twirl,
Where jellybeans giggle and whirl.

Whisked away on a vanilla breeze,
Where laughter bubbles, and everyone flees.
In spiced tales of wonder, we find our fate,
With tasty giggles, let's celebrate!

When Marshmallows Soar

Marshmallows take to the sky,
With gummy bears flying high.
Candy canes dance around,
A sweet circus on the ground.

Chocolate rivers flow with glee,
Lollipop trees sway merrily.
A parade of treats in the air,
Cakes with confetti everywhere!

Sprinkle fairies sprinkle bright,
While cupcakes giggle in the light.
Jelly beans jump, a wild spree,
Making friends with a buzzing bee.

As frosting clouds drift by,
And jelly rolls take to the sky,
Who knew sweets could be so spry?
In this land, joy will never die!

Secrets of the Sugar Plum Grove

In a grove where gumdrops grow,
Lollipop blossoms put on a show.
Whispers of fudge fill the air,
While licorice vines twirl without care.

Sassy squirrels steal a treat,
Chocolate acorns, oh what a feat!
Marzipan critters plotting schemes,
Living their sugary, sweet dreams.

Beneath the frosting-covered trees,
Countless secrets carried by the breeze.
Candy critters play hide and seek,
In this grove where giggles peak.

Smoke of cinnamon swirls around,
As gingerbread houses stand proud.
Join the fun, oh won't you see,
Sugar plum whispers set you free!

A Bakery of Beliefs

Welcome to the bakery bright,
Where pastries spin in pure delight.
Bakers in aprons that sparkle and shine,
Whisking up dreams with a dash of time.

Tarts singing tunes about love,
Croissants that swoop like a dove.
Every cookie has a tale to tell,
Of laughter and joy, oh so swell!

Sifting flour with giggles galore,
Snickerdoodle elves knocking at the door.
Pies that jump and jive,
In this bakery, we thrive!

Whipped cream clouds float overhead,
While sugar mice dance instead.
In this place where dreams take flight,
Laughter and sweets make everything right!

The Magic of Spiced Delights

Come gather round, oh friends so dear,
For a tale of joy and cheer.
In a pantry where spices play,
Funny flavors dance and sway.

Cinnamon sticks with hats so tall,
Whisking memories in a spice hall.
Ginger snaps in a merry parade,
Baking up laughter, never afraid.

Nutmeg whispers secrets sweet,
While green peppers join the beat.
Every jar holds a quirky story,
Flavors swirling, oh what a glory!

As baking magic fills the air,
With every stir, we all declare:
In this world of spiced delight,
Funny moments make it all feel right!

The Honeycomb Heart

A bee with a bowtie brings gifts on a tray,
Chocolate-covered giggles, we eat them all day.
Sticky fingers dancing, all over the floor,
Honeycomb surprises keep us coming back for more.

Rainbow sprinkles raining, just like confetti,
Lollipops in hand, we waddle and we're petty.
With candy-floss clouds floating high in the air,
A heart made of sweetness, no worries or care.

Whirlwind of Sweets and Surprises.

A carousel spins made of cupcakes and glee,
Candy canes dancing around a big tree.
Marshmallow mountains with jellybean streams,
We giggle and tumble, lost in our dreams.

Gummy bears giggling, they bounce without pause,
Chocolate-chip cookies distract us with their jaws.
Lemon drops laughing as they twirl in the sun,
In this whirlwind of sweets, we all have such fun!

Sugar-Spun Dreams

A castle of candy with turrets of cream,
Fairy tales told in a flavorful theme.
Licorice pathways that lead me around,
In a tapestry tasty, joy can be found.

Sugary whispers float high through the trees,
Tickling our toes in the soft morning breeze.
With each silly giggle, my heart starts to glow,
In a world made of sweetness where anything goes.

The Sweetness of Memory

Old-fashioned lollies and gumdrops so bright,
Remind me of laughter that lasts through the night.
Whimsical recollections of days filled with cheer,
The taste of nostalgia is sweet and sincere.

Each candy-coated moment, like bubbles in air,
Brings back the joy, a whimsical flair.
A gingerbread journey, forever we'll roam,
In a land full of sweetness, it's always our home.

Caramelized Wishes

A chef with dreams like candy clouds,
Stirring up laughter, drawing big crowds.
With chocolate rivers and gummy trees,
He chuckles and juggles, too full of glee.

His oven sings songs of cinnamon sweets,
While sprinkles of giggles dance on the streets.
A lollipop kingdom with marshmallow guards,
Creating a world that's all about shards.

When cookies start talking, they share all their jokes,
As licorice whispers, and sugar-glazed croaks.
Flavors collide in a marvelous mix,
With frosting that tickles, giving sweet kicks.

With every baked treat, the joy multiplied,
The chef in his hat was eccentric with pride.
So come take a bite, let the fun really start,
In this land of delights, where candy's the heart.

The Magical Mixer

In a kitchen of whimsy, the mixer spins round,
Mixing up giggles, with a whirring sound.
It twirls and it swirls, all flavors unite,
Creating concoctions that taste just right.

Sifting through powder that dances like fairies,
Buttercream dreams with chocolate cherries.
The bubbles of laughter, they float in the air,
As the mixer creates without a single care.

With a sprinkle of nonsense and dollops of fun,
Each batter is sizzling, like rays from the sun.
It croons little songs, as the cookies get baked,
And giggles are served on a plate that they make.

So grab a whisk, join in the play,
In this magical kitchen, we'll frolic and sway.
For who wouldn't want to whisk up some cheer,
In a land where sweet joy is always near?

Sweet Serenade of Spice

A journeyman baker named Billy McWhisk,
Wanders through flavors, a sweet little risk.
With frosted adventures and powdered delight,
He sings to the cookies beneath the moonlight.

Nutmeg plays trumpet, while cinnamon shouts,
As gingerbread men form a band that's what's spouted.
A cupcake extravaganza, a carnival scene,
Each pastry a note in a sweet serenade's dream.

Donuts are twirling, in rhythmic ballet,
While macarons giggle, swaying gay.
The marzipan maestro conducts from on high,
With a flourish of icing that flies through the sky.

When the sprinkles all shower down from above,
The cake gets a chance for a dance with a dove.
Sweet laughter erupts in a harmonized cheer,
In this festival of flavors, there's nothing to fear.

The Cozy Confectioner

In his snug little shop, the confectioner grins,
Crafting up delights, where the fun never thins.
With chocolate fondue and caramel streams,
He brews sugary jokes that burst into beams.

Marshmallow pillows, as soft as can be,
Add giggles and joy in whimsical spree.
Lollipops twirl in a jolly parade,
As candied carnations are lovingly made.

His whisk dances chaotically in flight,
Beneath twinkling lights that glow warm and bright.
With every sweet treat, a chuckle is stirred,
In a world made of whimsy where laughter's the word.

So come take a seat, and savor the cheer,
In this cozy corner, where sweets draw you near.
For in every bonbon, a smile's embedded,
A place where joy's found and giggles are threaded.

A Patchwork of Pastries

In a town where sweets do thrive,
Cookies dance, and cupcakes jive.
Brownies bounce on frosting floors,
Muffins prance through sugary doors.

Sour candies play hide and seek,
Jelly beans giggle, feeling cheek.
Gumdrop hills are steep and tall,
Lollipop trees sway, having a ball.

Pies spin tales with flaky crust,
While pastries whisper, 'In us, trust!'
Marshmallow clouds drift low, so fluffy,
As pies toss sprinkles, getting all huffy.

Then comes a baker, wild and spry,
Whipping up chaos, oh my, oh my!
With flour clouds and a twinkling eye,
He makes sweet magic, oh wouldn't you try!

The Lusciously Lost Recipe

In a book of treats, a page went missing,
Chocolate crumbs left quite a hissing.
Cakes turned to ghosts; they floated away,
Leaving muffins to wander and play.

Pies plotted a heist for the missing cream,
With fruit as their leader, a berry dream.
Cupcakes wore capes, ready to fly,
While cookies were dreaming of a big pie.

'Where's the butter?' shouted a roll,
As ginger snaps formed a sugary patrol.
Whiskers and winkles, laughter ensued,
As pastries planned their dessert-filled feud.

They searched high and low, with a curious plea,
For a recipe lost in the land of glee.
With giggles and wiggles, they danced to the beat,
Swearing one day they'd all taste that treat!

Frosted Footprints

Frosty footprints lead the way,
To a patch of sweets where children play.
Marzipan ducks quack out a song,
While gingerbread men jog along.

Curly straws twirl in the frosty air,
Noodles of icing, swirly and rare.
Candy canes march in a line so neat,
As the scent of fudge fills the street.

Backyards of donuts, frosted and wide,
Where gummy bears giggle and chomp with pride.
A lollipop dog runs after a cat,
Made of sweet taffy, how about that?

Every step crunches in sweetness divine,
Adventures are waiting, so colorful, fine.
If you follow the trail of the sugary cheers,
You'll uncover the joys of whimsical years!

A Symphony of Sugar

There's a concert of candy in the night,
With gummy bears playing till the morning light.
Marshmallows fluff, keeping rhythm and beat,
While chocolate drops dance with tiny little feet.

The licorice trumpet toots low and sweet,
As candied oranges tap their juicy feet.
Sugar sprinkles rain from the sky,
Creating a melody that makes you sigh.

Caramel violins, smooth and bold,
Gelato strings shimmer like gold.
Each note rises, a sugary cheer,
A symphony of sweetness we all hold dear.

As the audience cheers, they're stuck in delight,
Gazing at gumdrops glowing so bright.
In this sugary hall, laughter takes wing,
Join in the chorus, just let your heart sing!

Sweetness that Defies Time

In a world where candy grows,
Bubblegum trees and jellybeans close.
Lollipops bloom with a twisty cheer,
Chocolate rivers flow, never fear.

Marshmallow clouds float on by,
Gummy bears dance and sing up high.
Frosting falls like a pink snowfall,
Giggles erupt, oh, hear their call!

Licorice bridges span the lakes,
Underneath, a gumdrop shakes.
Candy canes build a merry place,
Everyone here wears a sugary face.

Time stands still, in this delight,
Silly sweets, all day and night.
The fun never ends, it's pure divine,
So grab a treat, and make it thine!

Beneath the Caramel Skies

Beneath skies of sticky gold,
Toffee tales of mischief told.
Nutty squirrels on licorice trees,
Jumping about in the honeyed breeze.

Chewy paths made of taffy strands,
Gingerbread folks with sugar bands.
Bouncing on gumdrops, such a sight,
They giggle and twirl with sheer delight.

Pudding puddles where puddles splash,
Fudge fountains flowing with a rush.
The sweetness here is hard to resist,
Every corner you turn brings a twist!

Let's skip along this tasty road,
With jellybean pals, we'll lighten the load.
Life is a party, just take a bite,
Under these caramel skies, all feels right!

A Realm of Icing and Hope

Enter a land of frosted dreams,
Where icing flows in lovely streams.
Cupcake mountains rise so high,
With sprinkles scattered in the sky.

Silly rabbits made of cream,
Twitching noses, what a theme!
Sipping tea from gumdrop cups,
Icing smiles while the laughter erupts.

Every corner, a sweet surprise,
Candy castles that mesmerize.
Dancing penguins, all dressed in fudge,
Join in the fun, you can't begrudge.

Hope is sweet, like peppermint swirls,
As we twirl with jolly little girls.
In this delight, we find our scope,
A realm alive with icing and hope!

Serenade of the Sugarplum Dancers

When night falls down with a sugary glow,
Sugarplum dancers steal the show.
Twirling on sprinkles, they leap and spin,
With giggles that make the moonlight grin.

Taffy curtains sway in the breeze,
Candy cane flutes play sweet melodies.
Peppermint twirls and marzipan bends,
Where every mischief simply transcends.

Encore calls for the jellybean band,
Playing tunes made of sugar so grand.
Lollipop lights dazzle the night,
As the world turns colorful and bright.

Oh, join this dance, it's all in good fun,
Under starry skies, until we're done.
Their laughter echoes, it's pure romance,
In this sweet serenade, take a chance!

The Twilight Tart

In the oven, tarts do dance,
Flavors swirling, take a chance.
Cherry giggles, lemon sighs,
Pastry moons in sugary skies.

Whiskers of cream, a playful twirl,
Jellybeans in a bright swirl.
Laughter echoes, crumbs take flight,
A funny feast in the cool twilight.

Gingersnap cousins join the fun,
Cinnamon whispers, "Oh what a run!"
With frosting hats and candy canes,
Silly smiles, ignore the stains.

As the tart cools, a show begins,
Cake pops leap, each one grins.
In this kitchen, joy's attire,
Tarts and laughter, never tire.

Revelry of the Sugar Sea

Candy boats set sail at noon,
Marshmallow waves dance to a tune.
Lollipop sails in vibrant hues,
Chocofish laugh, there's fun to choose.

Captain Jellybean takes the helm,
Bubblegum whales play in this realm.
With every splash, a smile appears,
The Sugar Sea is full of cheers.

Gummy sharks in a jolly chase,
Caramel tides, a sweet embrace.
Soda pop waves crash on the shore,
Joyful laughter, what's not to adore?

The sun sets low, in sprinkles we trust,
A land of sweets, it's a must!
In this sea, we sail with glee,
The revelry flows, oh can't you see?

Moonlit Marzipan Musings

By the moon, marzipan dreams,
Nutty thoughts in chocolate streams.
Fancies float on nougat skies,
Sugar-coated, giggles rise.

Rabbits made of almond paste,
Twirl and whirl, no time to waste.
Giggling fairies dance at night,
Under stars, oh what a sight!

Whispers of frosting, secrets be told,
Golden sprinkles, bright and bold.
Every bite, a tale to share,
Of sugar moons and tasty air.

So grab a friend, enjoy the call,
In this sweet land, we'll have a ball.
Marzipan musings, laughter's the theme,
In the moonlight, let's all dream.

The Home of Sugar Dreams

In a cottage of confection, sweet and bright,
Where gumdrops shine with pure delight.
Choco doors and candy walls,
Laughter echoes through the halls.

The roof's a crisp of toffee glaze,
With licorice vines in a joyous maze.
Inside, the treats are dancing free,
Sugar sprites sing, "Join the spree!"

Cupcake chairs and lollipop lights,
Silly songs on sugary nights.
Candy canes swirl in every room,
Filling the air with sweet perfume.

In this home, worries take flight,
With every treat, hearts feel light.
So come and wander, laughter beams,
Welcome friend, to sugar dreams!

Pastry Forest Secrets

In a forest made of sweets,
Choco trees sprout by the seats.
Candy critters burst with glee,
Whispering secrets by the pea.

Gummy bears dance in the night,
With jellybeans holding tight.
Silly squirrels in frosting hats,
Play peek-a-boo like fluffy cats.

The cookie crumb path leads the way,
To a cupcake palace that's here to stay.
But beware the licorice vine,
It tries to snack on your candy line!

So skip through the fields of melted joy,
Where sweet dreams await each girl and boy.
With sugar clouds lighting the air,
Mischief awaits, if you dare!

Frosting on the Horizon

Look, there's frosting on the hill,
Swirling patterns, what a thrill!
Marshmallow fluff drapes like a shawl,
Calling kids one and all.

A sprinkle storm brews up above,
Bursting cookies with a shove.
Candied rain falls soft like snow,
Covering everything in a glow.

Pies spin round in dizzy dances,
Baked goods offer sweet romances.
Everyone's grin stretches wide,
As pastries cuddle side by side.

In this land of fluffy dreams,
Life is sweeter than it seems.
With jelly toads on every route,
Laughs and giggles are never out.

Cocoa-Kissed Horizons

Cocoa beans at dawn's first light,
Bubbling pots that are a sight!
With chocolate rivers flowing free,
Join the fun, come swim with me!

A muffin tower sways and creaks,
Scones in hats with silly peaks.
The air is ripe with buttery smells,
While nearby the candy apple dwells.

Wobbling jellies spill and glide,
Racing marshmallows bump and ride.
Join the race, don't be too slow,
As licorice snakes slide to and fro.

Giggles echo through the dark,
As cherry blossoms miss their mark.
In this world of frosted cheer,
Laughter's song is all you'll hear!

Lollipop Labyrinths

Lost in a maze of twirling treats,
With lollipops as towering feats.
Twists and turns at every bend,
Where gummy worms eagerly pretend.

Every corner calls with a grin,
You can taste the fun within.
Chocolate walls invite the brave,
But is this a funhouse or a cave?

Brightly colored paths unwind,
A licorice cat, what will you find?
Steer clear from the taffy trap,
Or you'll take an unexpected nap!

Silly squeals fill the air,
In this land, none hold despair.
With every step, your heart will sing,
In candy wonder, joy takes wing!

Sugar-Coated Adventures

A frosted trail leads us near,
Where gumdrops dance and cheer.
Chocolate rivers flow with glee,
Caught in a lollipop spree.

The ginger snaps snap with delight,
As we takeoff in the night.
Willy Wonka's secret door,
Opens to a candy score!

Marshmallow clouds float so high,
With jellybean birds that fly.
Licorice whips swing us around,
While sugar fairies are found!

A cupcake castle stands so bright,
Frosting towers built with might.
Let's jump in that cherry pie,
Where giggles swirl and sugar flies!

The Melodrama of Marzipan

A marzipan princess sighs,
As her chocolate bear just flies.
They practiced their waltz all night,
But fell in a fudge-filled fright!

With a gumdrop crown on head,
She cried, "This is not how it's led!"
Yet sprinkles flew in the air,
While peanut brittle showed no care!

Candy canes play their strange tune,
Underneath a sugar moon.
The drama thickens like treacle,
As cookies fight like happy people!

Marzipan, the queen of sweets,
Dances away on sugary beats.
In this land of outrageous dreams,
Even gummy bears try to scheme!

Candytopia Awaits

Step right up to Candytopia,
Where chocolate cows moo with euphoria!
Jellybean fields stretch afar,
Underneath a caramel star.

The licorice bridge is long and sweet,
Where every candy lover meets.
Peanut butter puddles we leap,
As taffy twirls in dreams of sleep.

Cotton candy clouds puff white,
A merry-go-round of pure delight.
Bubblegum balloons float by,
Waving hello as we sigh!

In this land of endless fun,
Every second bursts like a bun.
So grab a cone and don't delay,
Candytopia's here to stay!

The Bakery Beneath the Stars

At midnight, the ovens hum,
As pastries dance and drums go thrum.
A bakery that never sleeps,
Where doughnut dreams make giggles leap!

Under stars like sprinkles bright,
Cookies do the cha-cha right.
Baker bears wear aprons grand,
Whisking magic with their hand!

The oven's door swings wide and warm,
As cupcakes twist in sugar swarm.
A breeze of vanilla fills the night,
While macarons take playful flight.

The night is young, the fun's a blast,
With frosting castles built so fast.
In this sweet shop of delight,
Every laugh is pure and bright!

The Chocolate Chip Chronicles

Once in a cookie, a chip went for a swim,
He splashed in the dough, feeling quite slim.
He called out to others, "Come join the tide!"
But the dough just laughed, "You can't run and hide!"

With sprinkles like stars, they danced on the tray,
Baking their fates in a sugary play.
"Jump high like a muffin!" the cookie did cheer,
But he plopped in the oven, and vanished in here!

A doughy adventure, full of glee,
With frosting and laughter, as sweet as can be.
The chips took the plunge, in a whirl and a whirl,
"Don't let the sugar-coated fate make you twirl!"

Once golden and crisp, they wiggled with flair,
"Let's make a parade!" they shouted, aware.
Then a whisking wind blew, the oven door cracked,
And the chip's dreams of dancing were totally whacked!

Holiday Hearth

Cozy flames crackle, like laughter in cheer,
Marshmallows giggle, the end of the year.
Stockings are stuffed with sweets and delight,
As we dance 'round the tree, till the end of the night!

Rudolph's red nose flickers, he'd stolen a scone,
When someone shouted, "That's really a bone!"
Cookies don't notice, they've started to snicker,
As frosting gets messy, these treats only flicker!

Cinnamon stars twinkle, a show on the wall,
As a gingerbread man takes a tumble and fall.
The laughter erupts, oh what a surprise!
A powdered sugar landing, right under the pies!

Sipping hot cocoa, with giggles all round,
Caught in the midst of this whimsied ground.
So gather your friends, without any fright,
Let's spice up the night till the morning light!

Candied Horizons

There once was a ginger who danced with a glee,
With jellybean shoes, she twirled like a bee.
Cotton candy clouds spun around her head,
As she leaped with joy on her sugar-cane bed!

A licorice path led to marshmallow lakes,
Where cupcakes sang songs, and the lollipop shakes.
"Let's race to the hills of the fudge-swirled delight!"
But she tripped on a gumdrop—oh what a sight!

Gummy bears chuckled as she rolled on the floor,
"Join us in laughter, there's always room for more!"
So off they all went, on their sweet-scented quest,
Laughing at mishaps, oh what a great fest!

Through rivers of caramel, they floated so free,
"This is the life, full of candy and glee!"
With smiles so wide, like a pie that's just baked,
They savored each moment, no calories to take!

The Meringue Monarch

In a kingdom of cream, a queen took her stand,
With meringue so fluffy, and a sweet little band.
Her crown made of chocolate, oh such a delight,
She ruled with a giggle—there's no end in sight!

Her subjects of cupcakes all bowed with a grin,
While jellybeans jiggled, let the fun begin!
"Let them eat pastries!" her motto declared,
As the frosted opponents felt slightly impaired.

A pie-eating contest, they hopped in a line,
As the ingredients jumbled, like a cake gone awry.
With spritzers and drizzlers, they caused quite the ruckus,

For the meringue monarch was truly miraculous!

The royal parade, made of cookies and cream,
Danced down to the bakery, fulfilling each dream.
With giggles and joy, she twirled round and round,
In a whimsical world where sweet smiles abound!

Marzipan Memories in the Twilight

In the twilight's playful glow,
Marzipan mice run to and fro,
With licorice tails and jellybean shoes,
Dancing around in sweet little blues.

Sunset sprinkles the sky with delight,
Chocolate rivers shimmer so bright,
As gumdrop trees sway in the breeze,
Whispering secrets to honeyed bees.

Frosted castles rise in the haze,
Where peppermint knights wear candy canes as praise,
Chocolate chip cookies are held high in cheer,
Baking memories that linger near.

Laughter echoes with every sweet bite,
As marshmallow clouds drift into the night,
In this whimsical world, we gleefully trod,
Savoring every silly little odd.

The Scent of Sugar and Adventure

A whiff of sugar fills the air,
As chocolate bunnies leap without a care,
Fizzy soda streams bubble with glee,
Inviting all to join the spree.

Take a dip in syrupy lakes,
Where gummy bears throw jolly shakes,
Each splash adds laughter, each ripple a grin,
In this wonderland, let the fun begin!

Candy-coated paths twist and turn,
As marshmallow suns begin to burn,
Adventure awaits with every sweet scent,
On taffy boats, together we went.

So grab a friend, let's giggle and play,
In this sugary realm, forever we'll stay,
With giggles and joy, we're sure to find,
The scent of laughter, forever entwined.

Whispers of Ginger and Honey

Whispers of ginger fill the breeze,
With honeyed laughter among the trees,
As caramel critters join the choir,
Their sweet serenades never tire.

Beneath a candy cane archway so bright,
Chocolate sprites dance in pure delight,
With licorice wands, they cast silly spells,
Telling tales of candy-coated wells.

In the distance, looms a gumdrop hill,
Where sugary wonders give hearts a thrill,
Ticklish frostings cover the ground,
As whispers of sweetness swirl all around.

So come and join in this playful chase,
With ginger and honey, we fill the place,
Sharing the joy in every sweet tone,
In a quirky land that feels like home.

The Candy Cane Chronicles

Once upon a peppermint night,
Candy canes danced in pure delight,
They spun and twirled with frosty grace,
In this whimsical, sugary place.

A gumball band played a jolly tune,
As jellybeans bounced under the moon,
Each note was bright, each beat a treat,
Creating a melody that can't be beat.

With gingerbread folks sharing a laugh,
Trading sweet tales on a sugary path,
The chronicles grew with cada shared bite,
As laughter echoed in the sweet twilight.

So gather your friends and let's sing loud,
In candy cane realms, we're silly and proud,
With each whimsical moment, we joyously pen,
The tales of our treats, again and again.

The Flour Dust Chronicles

Once upon a time with flour in the air,
The kitchen exploded with quite the flair.
Baking up giggles, and cakes that flop,
Mom says, "Remember, no doughnuts to drop!"

The cookie monsters march, all in a line,
Sneaking for treats, oh they think they're so fine.
But sprinkles are slippery, and icing's a trap,
They slide like they're skating, then fall with a thud!
Splat!

With sugar mountains high and frosting seas,
The laughter erupts like bubbles in teas.
We made ginger men dance, they started to twirl,
Until one got stuck to a sticky swirl.

So here in the chaos, we giggle with glee,
In a sweet little grip on our sugar spree.
Come join the madness where sweets come alive,
In a world full of whimsy, we all sure thrive.

The Orchard of Sugarplums

In an orchard of sweetness where sugarplums grow,
The trees aren't just trees; they put on a show.
With peppermint branches, they sway and they dance,
Who knew fruits of laughter could give such a chance?

There's candy-coated chatter beneath the sun's glow,
As gumdrops roll free, down the sweet hill they go.
With each bounce they giggle, a sugary cheer,
Spreading joy in the land where fun takes the steer.

From lollipop flowers to jellybean bees,
Every gust of wind carries candy-sweet breeze.
The laughter is ripe, and the smiles are wide,
As we taste every moment that life does provide.

Pick all your favorites, it's a colorful spree,
The orchard of giggles is where we all be.
With plums made of sugar and jokes on each stem,
We bloom in the sweetness: what a sweet gem!

Daydreams of Frosted Joy

In houses of frosting where dreams swirl around,
Every corner's sugary, a magical ground.
The rooftops are marshmallows, fluffy and light,
With gumdrop outlines that shine in the night.

We dance on the pathway made of licorice vines,
Chewing up giggles, tracing silly lines.
Candy corn whispers secrets filled with delight,
While chocolate-chip stars twinkle bright in the night.

Sipping on soda from fountains that fizz,
Every bubble's a giggle, it's a fizzy whiz!
The laughter erupts in a sweet little cheer,
In daydreams of frost, nothing's ever unclear.

So join in the frolic of cupcakes and cream,
In a world full of sweetness, we made our own dream.
With every grand giggle, this joy will remain,
In frosted delight, we'll dance in the rain!

Candy Cane Letters

With candy cane letters all stacked on my desk,
Writing notes to the world feels like quite the quest.
Each swirl tells a story, a giggle or two,
I sent one to Santa, it bounced off a shoe!

The postman is chuckling as he takes his sweet time,
Delivering laughter, just like poetry rhyme.
With peppermint ink and a cherry-red pen,
Every letter's a laugh — let's do it again!

From gingerbread friends to the sprightly snowmen,
We're scribbling down joy; it's a fine little trend.
They dance with the frost as they whip through the air,
Sending candy cane letters to friends everywhere!

So gather your giggles, your sweets, and your smiles,
Let's pen down this fun for a million sweet miles.
In the land of the silly, let the laughter take flight,
With candy cane letters, everything's just right!

The Land of Sugary Fantasies

Once there lived a gumdrop knight,
His armor made of candy bright.
He rode a horse made out of cake,
Together they would make kids quake.

With rainbow rivers flowing near,
They splashed and laughed without a fear.
In cookie forests, they would play,
And trick those bears with sweet ballet.

A lollipop tree waved hello,
While jellybeans jumped to and fro.
Marshmallow clouds cushioned their fall,
In this land, they had a ball!

But watch your step near chocolate streams,
Or you might slip and lose your dreams.
With every sour patch they'd cheer,
Adventure waits, so draw near!

Enchanted Apron Tales

The chef wore an apron stitched with glee,
Baking cakes as high as a tree.
He mixed with sprinkles, whipped with flair,
And puffed up pastries filled with air.

His oven sang a jolly tune,
Baking cookies morning to noon.
He danced with pies upon the floor,
While ginger folks came in for more.

One cookie rogue slipped in a pie,
With a wink and a sneaky cry.
The chef just laughed, he didn't mind,
For chocolate bits were well-designed.

So gather 'round, let laughter rise,
In the kitchen where fun never dies.
With aprons twirling, joy so bright,
Every day's a sweet delight!

Frosted Fantasies

In the land where frostings flow,
Cupcakes dance while candies glow.
With icing rivers, smooth and wide,
The frosted dreams we cannot hide.

A silly bear with a sugary hat,
Rode on a muffin, imagine that!
They tango'd on tarts, a sweet duet,
With jellybean friends, no sign of fret.

The gingerbread men did cartwheels,
While chocolate mice spun on wheels.
Such frosted fun, a comical scene,
In fantasies that felt like a dream.

So grab your forks, don't be shy,
In this land, we'll reach for the sky!
Every bite a chuckle, every cheer,
With frosted fantasies, we persevere!

Taffy Temptations

In a town made of stretchy taffy,
Silly kids felt oh-so-happy.
They bounced like balls, so light, so spry,
Under candy clouds, they'd skip and fly.

A taffy twist could stretch for miles,
As giggles rang with sticky smiles.
They licked their fingers, chewed with glee,
In this wobbly world, how fun to be!

But watch out for a sticky trap,
Where giggly goblins take a nap.
They wake up quick with a candy snare,
Taffy monsters just love to share!

So lift your spirits, laugh out loud,
In taffy's embrace, we feel so proud.
With every chew, we find our way,
To sweet temptations and silly play!

Frosted Fantasies Under a Candy Sky

Beneath a sugary sky, all is bright,
Where gumdrops dance and glimmers of light.
Marshmallow clouds float fluffy and round,
In this wacky realm, silliness abounds.

Lollipop trees sway, their colors shout,
Candied critters prance, hopping about.
A chocolate river bubbles with glee,
While licorice fish swim wild and free.

Silly winds blow, with a giggle they tease,
Tickling the noses of candy-sweet bees.
Jellybean flowers bloom with delight,
Sprinkling smiles, vanishing fright.

So come share a laugh, don't you delay,
In this frosted wonder, let joy play.
Every treat has a tale, come take a bite,
In this funny, sweet land, all feels right.

Enchanted Edibles and Sugary Temptations

Once there was a pie, wobbly with glee,
With giggles and sprinkles, it danced with me.
Cookie critters blinked in surprised awe,
As cupcakes wobbled, each flaunting a flaw.

Brownie mountains rose, erupting with cheer,
Doughnut boulders rolled, no sign of fear.
Cheesecake puppies barked, chasing around,
In a world of sweet treats, fun truly abounds.

Sugar-coated dreams, so silly and silly,
Where candy canes twist, and laughter gets frilly.
Frosting rivers flow, so thick and so sweet,
While jellybean bunnies hop on their feet.

Frizzy fudge trees sway in the sun,
Where every munch is a giggling pun.
Come, join the fun in this sugary spree,
With laughter and treats, oh what glee!

The Biscuit Kingdom Awakes

In a kingdom of biscuits, all crisp and so grand,
A jelly prince waved his gooey hand.
Tart flans twirled in a dance on the hill,
While cookies with hats just learned how to chill.

Crusty castles rise with jellybean moats,
Royal pies sailing on bread-like boats.
Gingerbread knights with their frosting bright,
Set off for adventure, oh what a sight!

The gumdrop guards stand tall and stout,
Chasing away grumpy, sugary doubt.
Every muffin smiles, moist and round,
As joy fills the air, a fun-loving sound.

With rolling hills of crumbly delight,
The biscuit kingdom sparkles in light.
Join the celebration, it's quite the affair,
With pastries and giggles filling the air!

Tales from the Licorice Forest

Deep in the forest, where licorice twists,
Funny tales hide in sugary mists.
Gummy bears giggle as they race by,
Bouncing through bushes, oh my, oh my!

Peanut butter trees wave branches so wide,
While toffee sloths slide down with pride.
Candy corn critters peek from the roots,
They're crafting sweet stories in sugary suits.

Chocolate owls hoot with sugary glee,
As marshmallow fireflies light up the spree.
Sugar plum fairies flutter and swirl,
Dancing with joy in a twinkling whirl.

Every step in the forest is a sweet surprise,
In this land of laughter, under candy skies.
So take a deep breath, and stay for the show,
Tales of the forest, where giggles will flow!

Milton Keynes UK
Ingram Content Group UK Ltd.
UKHW021628011224
451755UK00010B/508